The

Written by John Parsons
Illustrated by Kelvin Hucker

Contents   Page

The Perfect Pet

With these characters . . .

Dr. Harvey Shaw

Lena Rovalov

The Perfect Pet

"He was going to build

After his last invention, Dr. Harvey Shaw is determined never to make another terrible mistake. But he discovers that a scientific genius just can't stop from brilliant thoughts! Surely, with *this* invention, he will become as famous as the greatest inventor of all time! Nothing could possibly go wrong—could it? With his Perfect Animal Technology, Dr. Harvey Shaw is about to create something that is *sure* to impress: the perfect pet!

he world's first perfect pet!"

Chapter 1.

Dr. Harvey Shaw wandered down the street, deep in thought. He was thinking about his latest experiment. Although Dr. Shaw was a brilliant scientist, somehow, his inventions never turned out quite the way he expected. His current endeavor was no different. He faced a real puzzle to solve his perplexing problem!

Dr. Shaw had been trying to invent stronger egg shells that would not break easily. Step one involved feeding his free-range research hens a special diet of crushed seashells and bones to make their egg shells harder.

"That was the easy part," thought Dr. Shaw, as he strolled along.

Step one of the trial had worked so well that Dr. Shaw couldn't crack open a single experimental egg, even with a hammer. The egg shells were as hard as concrete. Now he had to figure out a way to open the eggs!

Maybe he could make his hens lay eggs with screw-tops on them? A brilliant solution!

Dr. Shaw was most impressed with himself.

Too eager to wait until his hens laid eggs again, Dr. Shaw had bought four dozen eggs from his corner shop and was returning to his laboratory. He had been walking down the street trying to think of a solution to his problem. So he was concentrating on his eggs and not on his surroundings. Dr. Shaw didn't see the monstrous Rottweiler dog dragging its owner along on a leash.

At the very moment that Dr. Shaw stopped to cross the road to his laboratory, the dog leapt up behind him and barked wildly. Dr. Shaw was so startled that he dropped his cartons of eggs. Crunch! The four egg cartons hit the pavement! Dr. Shaw groaned as he saw the yellow gooey mess seep out onto the concrete.

As Dr. Shaw leaned over to pick up the egg cartons, the dog stood behind him, growling and baring its teeth.

It waited until Dr. Shaw was bent right over, then pounced!

"Ouch!" cried Dr. Shaw, jumping forward. "That hurt!"

The embarrassed owner rushed up to Dr. Shaw.

"I'm terribly sorry," she said, puffing and panting. "This Rottweiler's just too big for me to control."

"That's OK," said Dr. Shaw, rubbing his bottom. "I know exactly what it's like when things are out of control!" He remembered some of his earlier experiments.

After the Rottweiler's owner had apologized
again, and hurried off, Dr. Shaw managed to put
all the egg cartons, and most of the broken eggs,
back into his carry bag. Shuffling back to the
corner store to buy some more eggs, he noticed a
fluffy, gray Siamese cat sitting on a fence.

"Hello, Kitty," he said absent-mindedly.
"You're much nicer than that nasty dog, aren't
you?" He reached out to give the cat a friendly
scratch around the ears.

The gray cat arched its back and hissed at Dr. Shaw. One second too late, Dr. Shaw whisked his hand away. Twisting forward, the cat sank its claws into Dr. Shaw's hand.

"Ouch!" cried Dr. Shaw again, frowning at the cat. "That really hurt!" The cat just stared back at him, daring him to try again. Dr. Shaw was not having a good day with animals. He wondered if his hens would attack and peck him when he returned to his laboratory!

Trudging toward the corner shop, Dr. Shaw tried to concentrate on his egg-shell problem. But, slowly, a better, more interesting experiment formed in his mind. The boisterous Rottweiler and that snarling Siamese cat had given him an idea. Smiling his "I'm a *brilliant* inventor" smile, Dr. Shaw circled around and hurried to his laboratory. He really had thought of a stupendously brilliant invention this time! There was work to be done!

Chapter 2.

Back at his laboratory, Dr. Shaw scribbled in his notebook.

Under the heading of "Pets," Dr. Shaw had made two columns. On one side, he listed the positive characteristics of pets. On the other side, he listed the negative ones.

Positive Characteristics	Negative Characteristics
Pets:	Pets:
• Provide company.	• Can bite and scratch.
• Can be good friends.	• Need to be fed.
• Are loyal to their owners.	• Are expensive to take to the vet.
• Like to play with people.	• Need to be brushed and cleaned.
• Can guard property and protect houses and their owners.	• Mess up the house.
	• Carry fleas and other insects.
	• Carry germs and bacteria.
	• Do not live as long as people do.
	• Can't speak.
	• Don't come in very many colors.
	• Can sometimes be selfish.

Dr. Shaw looked at his lists and nodded. Just as he had suspected: there were far more points in the negative column.

Then, on another sheet of blank paper, Dr. Shaw began writing out his plan. This new project was even bigger and far more important, than the egg-shell experiments. Dr. Harvey Shaw would be famous after all! Dr. Harvey Shaw was undertaking a top-secret project. He was going to build the world's first perfect pet!

All day and most of that night, Dr. Shaw worked constantly. He wrote a list of all the materials and equipment he would need and drew diagrams and sketches of how the perfect pet might look, inside and out.

"I will call it 'Perfect Animal Technology'—PAT for short!"

The next day, at his favorite shop, Labs-R-Us, Dr. Shaw filled his shopping cart with the hundreds of gadgets, wires, glass eyes, and electronic parts that were on his list.

The checkout clerk was amused as she stared at Dr. Shaw's cart.

"Goodness," she said, scanning the barcodes on his purchases. "What on earth are you building this time, Dr. Shaw?"

Dr. Shaw folded his arms and smiled at the clerk.

"I can't tell you yet," he said, glancing around to make sure no one was listening. "It's top-secret."

The clerk sighed and looked bored. "That's what all the scientists who come here say," she said, rolling her eyes. The total appeared on the cash register.

"That will be $412.35, please," said the clerk when she had finished packing all the items. "Will you be paying with cash or using your Inventors' Union credit card?"

Chapter 3.

Once he had unpacked his shopping bags, Dr. Shaw started constructing PAT. First, he built three small cameras that could be hidden in cute, brown glass eyes. He needed three, because he was going to have one at the rear, facing backwards. A pet that could see in two directions at the same time would be much more useful than one that could see only what was happening in front of it. People who needed guide dogs to help them walk around would find that *very* useful, he thought cleverly.

Then Dr. Shaw wove a special fabric fur that would last forever and never need cleaning. It could be easily sprayed with disinfectant to keep germs, fleas, and pests off it. It felt as soft as a cat's fur. Even better, it could be manufactured in any color. If purple was a person's favorite color, he or she could order a purple PAT pet. PATs would come in every color of the rainbow—even plaid!

"Ordinary pets are so dull," thought Dr. Shaw. "Cats come only in black, brown, white, or calico."

Dr. Shaw chose a striking green, blue, and red plaid for his first perfect pet.

Then he developed a microcomputer that would be the PAT pet's brain.

He worked for many days on the software that would control PAT's behavior. After checking his 'Positive Characteristics' list, Dr. Shaw programmed the microcomputer to make PAT loyal, playful, friendly, and protective.

Dr. Shaw controlled his microcomputer from a little black remote-control device similar to the one he used for his TV.

Later in the week, Dr. Shaw inserted a small loudspeaker in the perfect pet's throat. A tiny CD-ROM in its neck stored useful things that the perfect pet could say.

Instead of barking annoyingly, the perfect pet could say, "Hello. I will always be your friend, wherever you are," in a soothing voice.

Instead of meowing tunelessly, the perfect pet could say, "I would be happy to play with you," in a melodious voice.

"This is great!" exclaimed Dr. Shaw when he had finished. "Never again will the world be filled with pets that become bored or distracted from their main job—to keep their owners happy!"

Finally, after two months of concentrated work and many more visits to Labs-R-Us, Dr. Harvey Shaw was ready to test PAT. He closed all the blinds and curtains in his laboratory. To be sure of complete privacy, he locked the door and took the telephone off the hook. No one must see his top-secret experiment or disturb him while he was testing his ingenious invention!

Once PAT was placed up on the laboratory table, Dr. Shaw opened a small panel on its back. With excitement and wonder, he flicked the "on" switch!

Slowly, the perfect pet's eyes lit up. *Whirr! Click!* The microcomputer started up and loaded its software. The perfect pet grew warmer as the tiny heaters in its fur brought it to the right temperature. Then the two tiny eye cameras in the front of the perfect pet's head swiveled quickly and zoomed in and out on Dr. Harvey Shaw.

Dr. Shaw checked the eye camera at the back of PAT's head. Everything was functioning perfectly —so far. He held his breath. Would PAT really be perfect?

Chapter 4.

Success! The perfect pet's tail started to wag. Like a young child being offered a new toy, Dr. Shaw jumped up and down and clapped his hands with glee. He had created the perfect pet! Never again would the world be the same! Never again would people have to put up with boring, *real* animals. He, Dr. Harvey Shaw, would be famous at last!

Dr. Shaw picked up PAT's remote control and pressed a button with a walking symbol on it. The perfect pet walked to the edge of the table and leapt off. Landing on the floor gracefully, it pressed itself up against Dr. Shaw's legs. PAT made a friendly purring sound like a cat.

Dr. Shaw pressed another button with a mouth symbol.

The loudspeaker in the perfect pet's throat crackled and boomed.

"I WOULD BE HAPPY TO PLAY WITH YOU," shouted the perfect pet. The laboratory windows rattled and Dr. Shaw was startled by the deafening noise. He quickly adjusted the volume on the remote control.

This time, when he pressed the voice button, PAT spoke in a quieter voice.

"I would be happy to play with you," it said, its electronic tail wagging.

Dr. Shaw jumped up and down again and did a little dance. It was lucky all the blinds and curtains were closed! He felt so exhilarated he wanted to rush out and tell everyone about his remarkable new invention. But Dr. Shaw knew he had to conduct more tests before he could inform the rest of the world about the arrival of PAT, the perfect pet.

Dr. Shaw continued to tinker and tap on the perfect pet, making tiny adjustments to the way it operated. He rewrote parts of the software so that the perfect pet behaved even more like a real animal—but, of course, without any of its annoying habits, like biting or scratching. Dr. Shaw programmed it to observe the things that people liked to do and to imitate them. Finally, when he had completed his adjustments, he phoned his girlfriend, Lena Rovalov.

"Lena!" he said excitedly when she answered the phone. "I have some wonderful news!"

"That is good!" she said in a thick Russian accent. "What have you done?"

"I can't tell you," he whispered secretively. "Come over for dinner and I'll show you."

"I won't tolerate another dangerous meal!" she said vehemently. "Remember our last picnic? Oh, those extremely hard-boiled eggs!"

Lena had been trying to crack open one of Dr. Shaw's rock-hard experimental eggs with a hammer when it fell and broke her little toe.

"No, no," Dr. Shaw assured her. "I've stopped the egg-speriments. This is far more important!"

"I will see you at six o'clock, then," replied Lena. Dr. Shaw hung up and rushed back into the laboratory.

He tripped and fell over the blue, green, and red tartan object waiting at his feet.

"I would be happy to play with you," sang the perfect pet, wagging its tail happily. A long, wet tongue darted out of PAT's mouth and licked Dr. Shaw's face as he lay helplessly on the floor.

Dr. Shaw smiled, wiped his face with the sleeve of his laboratory coat, and picked himself off the floor.

"Good PAT," he said, stroking the perfect pet. "Now, follow me. We have to fix you up so you look perfect for Lena."

Dr. Shaw and PAT trotted back to the laboratory looking extremely pleased with themselves.

By the time Lena arrived, at exactly six o'clock, Dr. Shaw had entered even more information into the microcomputer about the way a perfect pet should behave. PAT happily followed him around everywhere.

Lena gasped when Dr. Shaw opened the door.

"What is *that*?" she asked in a frightened voice. She pointed shakily at the perfect pet.

"That," stated Dr. Shaw proudly, "is PAT, my perfect pet."

Lena looked at Dr. Shaw in amazement.

"Oh, Harvey," she cried. "You are so brilliant! What an exceptional scientist you are."

She reached down to stroke the perfect pet.
PAT jumped backwards, and its tiny cameras
swiveled and whirred as they focused on Lena.

"Unidentified intruder!" it growled menacingly.
"I must protect my master!"

PAT crouched down, ready to pounce. Long
claws appeared from its mechanical paws.
Nervously, Lena backed away. Dr. Shaw quickly
fumbled for his remote control and pressed a
button with a smiling face on it.

"Sorry, Lena. It still needs a few more minor
adjustments," he apologized, looking quite
embarrassed. "It was only trying to protect me."

"Hmm," mumbled Lena.
She did not look impressed.
She eyed the perfect pet warily.
It wagged its tail.

"I would be happy
to play with you."

"Maybe,"
muttered Lena.
"But *I* don't
want to play
with *you!*"

Dr. Shaw laughed and followed Lena down the hallway. "Don't worry, Lena," he said reassuringly. "You'll get used to it. And it will get used to you."

After dinner, Lena and Dr. Shaw relaxed on the couch.

"Now, let me demonstrate what else PAT can do," said Dr. Shaw. "I've programmed it to behave just like a cat or a dog—but without the nasty habits that real animals have." He pressed a command button on his remote control, and PAT sat up on its hind legs and shook hands with Dr. Shaw.

Lena raised an eyebrow. She looked warily at the perfect pet. She was still not convinced that this invention was a good idea.

Dr. Shaw pressed another command button. The perfect pet raced out of the room and, a few seconds later, returned with a newspaper between its teeth.

Lena knew that Dr. Shaw was delighted with his perfect pet, so she thought she had better compliment him.

"Well, my wonderful scientist, if you like PAT, then I am happy for you." She leant over to kiss him on the cheek.

The perfect pet watched what Lena was doing, and its microcomputer whirred and clicked. Instantly, it jumped up on the couch and licked Lena's lips with its long, wet tongue.

"Aaargh!" she screamed, spitting and coughing. "That *contraption* tried to kiss me!"

Dr. Shaw looked horrified. "It was only trying to imitate you," he said, trying to explain.

"Well, I do NOT need an imitation kiss from THAT!" she yelled, standing up and stomping out of the room. "I will see you next week. By that time, I hope you will have got rid of that ... that ... MONSTER!"

Dr. Shaw sat speechless as the door slammed.

"Oh, dear," he thought. "I've gained a pet and lost a girlfriend. Some reprogramming work must be done on PAT tomorrow."

Chapter 5.

While Dr. Shaw cleared away the dinner dishes, he thought about how he could improve PAT.

"It's late," he finally said wearily. He looked at his perfect pet affectionately and it stared back at him. "Tomorrow, we'll make you behave perfectly."

Dr. Shaw shuffled into his bathroom and ran a bath. When it was full, Dr. Shaw lay down in the warm, soothing water, closed his eyes, and imagined what a great place the world would be when everyone had a perfect pet. He had a big, satisfied smile on his face.

Suddenly, Dr. Shaw's eyes popped open as he heard whirring and whizzing beside the bath. Frantically, he reached for the remote control resting on his towel. Too late! The perfect pet made a huge, curving dive into the bath.

Splash! Water splashed all over the tiled floor. The perfect pet floated in the bath and stared up at Dr. Shaw.

"Hello. I will always be your friend, *wherever* you are," it gurgled.

Dr. Shaw groaned. He stood up and wrapped a dripping towel around himself, thanking his lucky stars that he had made PAT's electrical components waterproof! He picked up the soaking-wet perfect pet, which was steaming as the heaters in its fur evaporated the bathwater.

Dr. Shaw carefully placed PAT on the floor. Once he had finished drying himself off, he put on his pajamas. Feeling a little disappointed, he walked down the hall to the living room. But when he tried to shut the door, it was jammed. He looked down and the perfect pet stared back up at him.

"Hello. I will always be your friend, wherever you are."

Dr. Shaw felt exasperated. He pushed the perfect pet back out of the doorway with his foot, and the perfect pet's microcomputer whirred and clicked. A paw appeared around the corner of the door and pushed Dr. Shaw so hard that he almost fell onto the sofa. The perfect pet wagged its tail excitedly.

"I would be happy to play with you."

"LATER!" said Dr. Shaw angrily. As he tiptoed back to his bedroom, he hoped that the perfect pet wouldn't notice. But, from behind him, he could hear the gentle padding of four electronic paws and a low, purring sound.

Dr. Shaw grumbled. This perfect pet wasn't working out quite the way he had planned.

First, PAT had annoyed Lena. Then it had ruined his relaxing, peaceful bath. Then it wanted to push its way into the living room!

Dr. Shaw reached down and picked up PAT again, narrowly avoiding another great slurp across his face. He grabbed the remote control and shut his not-so-clever experiment in the laboratory.

Sighing with relief, Dr. Shaw returned to his bedroom and crawled into bed.

Just when he had turned off the light, he heard a scratching sound at the bedroom door.

"What now?" he groaned. He swung his legs out of bed and pushed open the door. "How did you get out?" he whispered. "Go *away* and let me sleep."

"I would be happy to play with you," replied a low, eager voice.

Dr. Shaw stared at the ceiling. With a sinking feeling, he realized that his pet was *not* perfect. PAT gave him *too much* companionship, friendship, loyalty, and protectiveness. It did not make him feel better. It demanded more attention than a real animal did. He worried that he would never have enough privacy to bathe, or sleep ever again with *that* machine following his every move.

Dr. Shaw made a difficult decision. He swung open the door and, quick as a flash, flipped open the control panel on the perfect pet's back. Before PAT had time to react, Dr. Shaw flicked the switch off. The perfect pet's eyes whirred and swiveled around. The tail wagged slower and slower. The purring grew quieter and quieter. The perfect pet lay down silently on the floor.

"At last," breathed Dr. Shaw with a sigh of relief. "I think I have finally learned my lesson. Things are *sometimes* best left exactly the way they are!"

Chapter 6.

In the morning, Dr. Shaw telephoned Lena to tell her the good news about discarding the perfect pet project. But she was still in a bad mood.

"Harvey, my dear," she scolded. "I'm afraid that you are too weird and wacky for me. I have decided that I will return to Russia for a long, long vacation. There, I will not have to pay doctors to fix my toes after your picnics. There, I will not have to kiss disgusting machines!"

"But, Lena," pleaded Dr. Shaw. "I promise I won't invent anything so ridiculous again."

"We shall see," said Lena in a huff. "Good-bye, Harvey. I shall see you in six months."

Dr. Shaw hung up the phone glumly. What would he do without Lena to talk to? He liked having her around and showing her his latest inventions and experiments.

Apart from being in a bad mood sometimes, she was ... well, she was almost perfect!

Suddenly, Dr. Harvey Shaw had a brilliant idea. It was better than the egg-shell idea. It was even better than the perfect pet idea!

At last, he would be known as the greatest scientist of his time. This latest idea was so brilliant that he wondered why no one had ever thought of it before! He put the telephone answering machine on, closed all the blinds and windows, and rushed into his laboratory.

Grabbing his pencil and notepad, he wrote a heading on a new page, and made two columns.

In the first column, he wrote:

- Must be able to play football.
- Must always like what I cook for dinner.
- Must understand my brilliant ideas.
- Must have a sense of humor.

Dr. Shaw chewed on the tip of his pencil, deep in thought. He looked again at his heading, tapped his feet and hummed a tune. This was going to be the most successful experiment ever!

In large, black letters, he had written:

"The Perfect Girlfriend."

"Perfect Animal Technology!"

Having learned from my mistake, I have vowed not to create
Another invention that the world would regret.
So I'll build myself a friend, upon whom I can depend.
I shall call him PAT, the perfect pet!

He'll have fur my favorite shade, wag the friendly tail I've made,
He will be a pal my whole life long.
Yes, I'm sure that in the end he'll be a true best friend,
I'm quite sure that nothing can go wrong!